Science
Success

2

Terry Jennings

OXFORD

UNIVERSITY PRESS

Acknowledgements

The author and publisher would like to thank the following for help in the preparation of this book:
Francis Baily Primary School, Thatcham; Manor County Primary School, Uckfield; Jeremy Cottam; Ann Mepham; Julia Ware; National Dairy Council; British Airways

Photographic credits
Bo'sun/R D Battersby pp 6, 9, 12 (top), 13, 14, 15 (top), 16, 17 (top, bottom), 19, 20, 26 (bottom), 27, 30 (top, bottom), 31, 35 /L R Miles p 37; courtesy of British Airways p 34; Bruce Coleman /Pacific Stock p 10 (bottom); James Davis Worldwide pp 12 (bottom), 22 (bottom); Eye Ubiquitous /Sean Aiden p 8 (top) /David Langfield p 21 /Charles W. Friend p 22 /John Wender p 44 (top); Terry Jennings pp 26 (top), 40 (top, bottom), 43, 44 (bottom); courtesy of National Dairy Council p 10 (top); Oxford Scientific Films /Eyal Bartov p 23 /David Cayless p 36 (top) /J A L Cooke p 41; P A Photos /David Jones p 8 (bottom); Science Photo Library /Jerrican/Faure Felix p 11 /Martin Bond p 15 (bottom).

OXFORD
UNIVERSITY PRESS

Great Clarendon Street, Oxford OX2 6DP

Oxford University Press is a department of the University of Oxford. It furthers the University's objective of excellence in research, scholarship, and education by publishing worldwide in

Oxford   New York

Auckland Cape Town Dar es Salaam Hong Kong Karachi Kuala Lumpur Madrid Melbourne Mexico City Nairobi New Delhi Shanghai Taipei Toronto

with offices in

Argentina Austria Brazil Chile Czech Republic France Greece Guatemala Hungary Italy Japan Poland Portugal Singapore South Korea Switzerland Thailand Turkey Ukraine Vietnam

Oxford is a registered trade mark of Oxford University Press in the UK and certain other countries

© Terry Jennings 2000

The moral rights of the author have been asserted

Database right Oxford University Press (maker)

First published 2000

20 19 18 17 16 15 14 13 12 11

ISBN 0 19 918339 2

ISBN 13: 9780199183395

Editorial, design and picture research by Lodestone Publishing Limited, Uckfield, East Sussex

Illustrations by Chris Duggan, Nick Hawken, Cathy Wood, and Dawn Brend

Science consultant Dr Julian Rowe

Language consultant Margaret Hawkins

Printed in Spain by Gráficas Estella, S.A.

Contents

(and suggested order of teaching)

Bones and skeletons

Inside your body you have a **skeleton** made of **bones**. Some animals have a skeleton on the outside of their body. The crab's shell is really a skeleton. As a crab grows too big for its shell, it has to shed its old shell and grow a new one. Your skeleton grows as you grow, so you will never get too large for your skeleton.

Skeletons are important

Your skeleton is important in many ways. It holds your body upright and gives it its shape and strength. Without a skeleton your body would be floppy, like an earthworm or a jellyfish. Neither of these animals has a skeleton! Your skeleton also protects delicate parts of your body. Your skull protects your brain, and your ribs form a cage that protects your heart and lungs. Safely inside your backbone is your delicate spinal cord. Your brain sends messages down the spinal cord to all parts of your body.

Bones

There are 206 different bones in the human skeleton. Some are long, some are short, and some have strange shapes. The thigh bone is the longest, and the smallest is one of the tiny bones inside the ear. It is about 3 mm long and weighs only 3 mg. Not all bones are solid. The long bones of your arms and legs are hollow. They are filled with a jelly-like substance called **marrow** which helps to make blood. If the long bones were not hollow they would be too heavy to move. A hollow bone is strong but light.

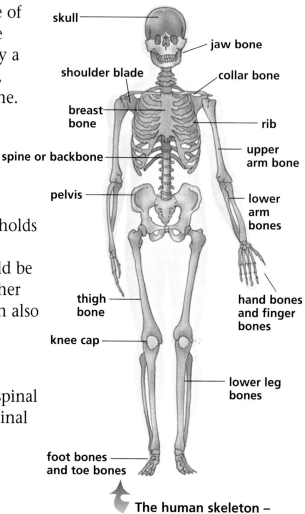

skull — jaw bone — shoulder blade — collar bone — breast bone — rib — spine or backbone — upper arm bone — pelvis — lower arm bones — thigh bone — hand bones and finger bones — knee cap — lower leg bones — foot bones and toe bones

The human skeleton – can you feel these bones in your body?

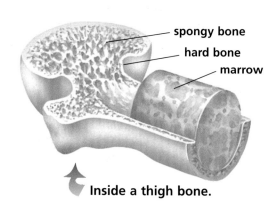

spongy bone — hard bone — marrow

Inside a thigh bone.

Living bone

Bone can be as strong as some kinds of steel. It is a living, growing substance, which is why a broken bone can grow and mend again.

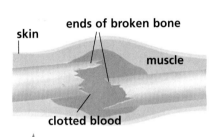

skin — ends of broken bone — muscle — clotted blood

bony swelling around the broken ends

slight swelling of the bone remains and the two ends have joined

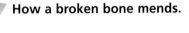

How a broken bone mends.

Questions

1 a Make your own skeleton out of thin card cut into the shapes of bones. Join them with string or paper fasteners.

  b Describe in your own words why your skeleton is important.

  c Find out all you can about the skeletons of other animals. How and why are they different from our skeleton?

2 The long bones of your arms and legs are hollow which makes them strong but light. Where else can you see hollow objects being used because they are strong but light?

3 a How many bones are there in your middle finger?

  b Which is the only part of your skull that you can move?

  c Whereabouts is the longest bone in your body?

  d What do we call the part of the body which joins the lower arm and upper arm bones?

  e How do doctors find out whether a bone is broken?

Muscles and movement

You can move your arms, legs, hands, fingers, toes and other parts of your body only because the bones have **joints** between them.

The power to move your bones comes from your **muscles**. Muscles pull on your bones to move them. Everyone has muscles and they make up about 40 per cent of the weight of your body.

Muscles pull

Muscles are quite soft. If you look at a piece of meat you can see muscle. The muscle is the lean, red part of the meat. Muscles need a lot of food and **oxygen** and the blood carries those substances to them. That is why lean meat, or muscle, is red.

Muscles can only pull. When a muscle pulls on a bone it becomes shorter and fatter. We say that the muscle **contracts**. To pull the bone back again, another muscle contracts. You can feel the muscle pulling your forearm and becoming shorter and fatter if you hold your arm like the boy in the photograph. Your arm is pulled straight again when the muscle at the back of your arm contracts. While it is doing this, the muscle at the front of your arm **relaxes** and becomes longer and thinner. Muscles always work in pairs like this. One muscle contracts while the other muscle relaxes.

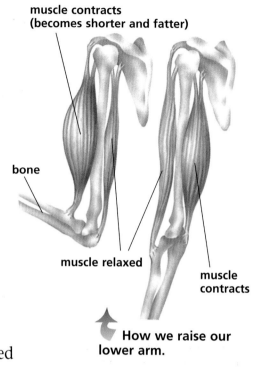

muscle contracts
(becomes shorter and fatter)

bone

muscle relaxed

muscle contracts

How we raise our lower arm.

The muscle at the front of your upper arm contracts to pull up your lower arm.

Tendons

Sometimes the bones you need to move are too far from the muscles to be attached to them. Then the muscle pulls on a cord called a **tendon**. The other end of the tendon pulls on the bone.

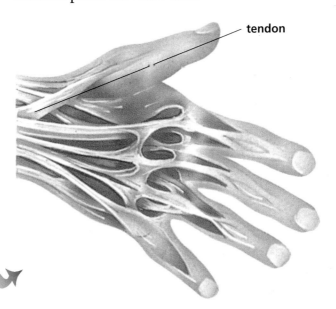

tendon

You need tendons in your hand because the muscles in the forearm are too far away from the finger bones to be attached to them.

Questions

1 Think about how a string puppet works.
   a In which ways is this similar to the way our bones and muscles work?
   b How is it different?

2 a How many different joints can you find in your body?
   b Draw a picture of yourself. Mark on it the joints you have found.
   c With a friend, talk about how these joints bend.

3 Make the movements listed below and use your hands to feel the muscles working. You may need to work with a friend. For each movement, draw a picture to show where the muscle is contracting (bulging) and where it is relaxing (becoming longer and thinner).
   a Pick up a heavy book and hold it in front of you with your arm straight.
   b Lift the book in your hand, but bend your arm at the elbow.
   c Stand on tiptoe and keep the lower part of your leg straight.

Exercise and muscles

You use your muscles all the time. You use muscles when you walk, run, smile or talk, and even when you sit still or sleep. This is because your heart is made of muscle and you use muscles to breathe. Some activities, like running, jumping or playing ball, make your muscles work very hard.

It is good for our bodies to make our muscles work hard.

Energy from food

The energy to make your muscles work comes from the food you eat. The heat energy to keep your body warm also comes from your food. Your body gets energy by burning up the food you eat. You burn up your food in your muscles. Your muscles use oxygen from the air you breathe in to slowly burn up food.

How does this weight-lifter make and keep his muscles strong?

Exercise and rest

Athletes have to train hard to strengthen their muscles.

When you exercise hard, you make your muscles work hard. Then they need more oxygen from the air you breathe in, so exercise makes you breathe faster. When you exercise, your heart also beats faster, pumping blood even more quickly than usual. That is how it is able to get more food and oxygen to your muscles.

Exercise is an important part of living. Exercise helps to keep you healthy and fit. It makes your muscles strong and active and develops your lungs. Because your heart is a muscle, it needs exercise too. If you do not take regular exercise, your muscles will get weak, but you cannot keep active all through the day and night. Your body and your muscles also need time to rest and recover. When you are asleep, your body rests, grows and repairs itself. Your muscles relax and your heartbeat and breathing slow down.

Questions

1 In your own words, explain what happens to your body when you exercise.

2 With your friends, plan and carry out some experiments to see how strong certain muscles are in your bodies.
   a How will you make your experiment fair?
   b What measurements will you make?
   c Which are the strongest muscles?

3 Everyone needs both exercise and rest if their bodies and minds are to work properly. Think about all the things you do each day or each week. Make a list of them.
   a Which of your activities need a lot of physical effort?
   b Which activities need a lot of mental effort, or concentration?
   c Which activities need both physical and mental effort?
Compare your lists with those of your friends.

Solids and liquids

Materials can be grouped in many ways. One way is to **classify** them as solids, liquids or gases. Scientists call these the three **states of matter**. You are a mixture of these states of matter. You have **solid** bones, teeth, fingernails and toenails. Your blood is a **liquid**, and you have a **gas** (air) in your lungs. In this unit we look at solids and liquids.

Liquids, such as milk, take up the shape of the container they are placed in.

Solids

Solids have a fixed shape, like a stone or a cup. Solid materials can be cut or shaped. When you pick up solids, they keep their shape, although they may break if you drop them.

Liquids

Liquids such as water and milk have no fixed shape. Liquids are runny and if you pour them into a container, they will take up the shape of the container. The surface of a liquid in a container stays level, but if you spill a liquid, it will flow all over the place.

Melting

Some solids can be turned into liquids quite easily by heating them. Ice cream, candle wax, chocolate, butter and margarine are solids, but they **melt** easily and turn to liquid if they are warmed. If you cool them, they turn back into solids. We say that these materials have low **melting points**. Similarly, it is quite easy to turn solid ice into liquid water by warming it. The water is turned back to solid ice by cooling it. This change from a liquid to a solid is called **freezing** or **solidifying**.

Liquid rock or lava comes from an erupting volcano. When the molten rock cools, it becomes a solid.

High melting points

Many solids have high melting points. You have to heat them a lot to melt them. We usually see metals such as iron, copper and gold as solids, but if you heat them enough they will melt and become liquids. Many pieces of jewellery and parts of machines are made by pouring liquid metal into moulds. The metal is allowed to cool and it sets hard in the shape of the mould.

Liquid (molten) metal is being poured into a mould to make a bell.

Questions

1 Make a list of all the solids and liquids you use in one day. Can any of the solids be changed into liquids?

2 How do solids and liquids behave differently? Explain it in your own words.

3 Copy each of the following sentences a–g. After each sentence write whether you think it is about solids or liquids.

a They stay the same shape and do not pour.
b They can melt when they are heated.
c They can freeze when they are cooled down.
d They have a flat surface when put in a container.
e You can sometimes cut them.
f They are usually hard to squeeze and they keep their own shape.
g They tend to run downhill.

Mixing solids and liquids

If you mix a solid and a liquid together, different things may happen. The solid may disappear in the liquid, or the solid may simply sink to the bottom of the liquid.

Dissolving

If you stir a teaspoonful of sugar in a glass of water, the sugar seems to disappear. If you drink a little of the liquid, you can tell that the sugar is still there because you can taste it. When the sugar disappears like this, we say it has **dissolved** in the water. The sugar has formed a **solution**. If the water is hot, more sugar will dissolve than if the water is cold. Even so, there comes a point when you cannot dissolve any more sugar. Sugar solution is a mixture of sugar and water.

Sugar crystals dissolve in water and form a solution.

The Dead Sea contains so much dissolved salt that you can float in it, even if you cannot swim.

Other solutions

Many other solids dissolve in water. Water is good at dissolving things. We say it is a good **solvent**. Seawater is a solution of different salts in water. In the soil, mineral salts dissolve in water and are later taken up by plants.

Cleaning

Dirty plates and dirty clothes are washed in water. The water loosens the dirt. Soaps or detergents are needed for the water to dissolve grease and stains. A hot, soapy solution is better than a cold one because it dissolves the grease and stains more easily.

Insoluble substances

Not all substances dissolve, even if hot water is used. If you shake up a little sand in a jar of water, the sand will not dissolve. Substances like sand, which will not dissolve in water, are said to be **insoluble** in water.

If you leave the jar to stand, the sand settles out at the bottom of the jar.

Questions

1 How can you make a spoonful of sugar dissolve faster? Write down two ways. Draw pictures to show what you would do. Write a caption for each picture that describes what is happening.

2 Plan an experiment to find out if coffee granules dissolve better in cold water or hot tap water, or if there is no difference.
  a Write down what you would do, what equipment you would use and what measurements you would take.
  b How would you make your experiment fair?

3 True or False? Copy each sentence. Write True if it is correct or False if it is wrong.
  a Sugar, salt and instant coffee dissolve in water.
  b Substances that do not dissolve in water are said to be soluble in water.
  c Sand does not dissolve in water.
  d There is no limit to how much salt or sugar will dissolve in water.
  e All solids dissolve better in cold water than in hot water.
  f Fizzy drinks contain dissolved gas.
  g Soaps and detergents help water to dissolve grease.

Separating solids from liquids

We can use a funnel and filter paper to separate sand from water.

You can get a dissolved solid substance back from a solution. You can also get insoluble substances back from a mixture with a liquid such as water.

Evaporation

If you put a little sugar solution in a clean saucer and leave it on a sunny windowsill, after a time the water will dry up or **evaporate**. The sugar from the solution will be left in the saucer. If you heat the solution, the water evaporates much more quickly and leaves the sugar behind.

It is possible to separate other dissolved substances from liquids in a similar way. If, for example, you heat a little seawater in a clean dish, the water soon evaporates. The salts dissolved in the seawater will be left in the dish.

Decanting

You can get some insoluble substances back from a mixture with a liquid by **decanting**. If the substance has settled at the bottom of a container, you can carefully pour away or decant the liquid, leaving the substance behind.

Filtering

Another way to separate an insoluble substance from a liquid is to use a **filter**. A filter is made of material which has many tiny holes in it. It is like a very fine sieve. A filter cannot be used to separate sugar which is dissolved in water because the particles of sugar are too small. A filter will separate the larger particles of sand or soil from water, though.

A tea bag is a kind of filter. It keeps the large tea leaves in, but allows the soluble parts of the tea to pass through.

At the waterworks, water is passed through thick layers of sand and gravel to filter out the dirt.

Questions

1 How would you separate a mixture of salt and sand?
   a Write down what you would use and what you would do.
   b Draw a picture of your experiment.
   c What do you think would happen?

2 If you look inside a kettle, you may see a white chalky substance. Think about where the water comes from before it gets into the water pipes, then answer the questions.
   a How do you think this substance gets into the kettle?
   b How could you stop this from happening?

3 In some countries there is a shortage of fresh drinking water, but there is often plenty of seawater. It is not possible to get the salt out of seawater by filtering. How could fresh water be obtained from seawater?

Temperature

The **temperature** of something is how hot or cold it is. We measure temperature using a thermometer.

Thermometers

This thermometer measures the hotness or coldness of the air. The liquid in the thermometer takes up more room when it is warmed. We say the liquid **expands**. The more the liquid is heated, the more it expands and rises up the tube.

When it is cooled, the liquid **contracts** or gets smaller. The more it is cooled, the more the liquid contracts and the further back down the tube it goes. So the level of the liquid in the thermometer changes with the temperature of the air.

Degrees

The temperature on a thermometer is shown in **degrees**. Each mark on the thermometer is one degree. Many thermometers have a **scale** with 100 marks. It is called the **Celsius scale** after Anders Celsius, the man who invented it. The temperature of boiling water is 100 degrees Celsius (100˚C), and water freezes at 0˚C on this scale.

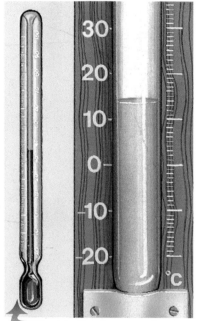

A wall thermometer is used to measure the temperature of the air.

High temperature.

Low temperature.

What is the temperature shown by these thermometers?

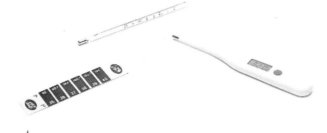

These thermometers are used to take the temperature of our body

Body temperature

Other kinds of thermometers are used to take your temperature if you are ill. These thermometers tell you the temperature of your body. Your temperature will be about 37°C when you are well. It will be higher than this if you are ill. Your temperature stays the same whether the day is hot (28°C) or cold (3°C). Your temperature stays the same whether you are in a hot bath (40°C) or in a cold one (10°C).

This thermometer is used to take the temperature of the soil.

Questions

1 Look at the objects listed in the box below. Some of these things are cold, some are warm, and some are hot. Write out the list putting the objects in order with the coldest first and the hottest last.

cup of tea	ice cube	goldfish bowl
glass of iced lemonade		electric iron
hot bath	electric fire	child

2 What will happen to a thermometer if you put it in a cold place and then in a warm place? Describe what happens in your own words. Draw two pictures to illustrate your descriptions.

3 It is important when you do a scientific experiment to make sure your test is fair. If you wanted to record the temperature outside on the playground every day for a week, how could you make sure your test was fair?

Thermal conductors and insulators

Some materials allow heat to pass through them easily. These are said to be good **thermal conductors**. Metals are good thermal conductors. That is why saucepans and kettles are made of metal. If you stand a metal spoon in a cup of hot drink the spoon quickly gets hot. The spoon conducts the heat from the drink to your fingers.

Insulators

Metals naturally feel cold when you touch them. This is because they carry the heat away from your fingers quickly. Some other materials feel warm when you touch them. Wood, plastic, cork, cloth and wool feel warm because they do not carry the heat away from your fingers quickly. They are said to be good **thermal insulators**.

What different materials are used to make this saucepan?

What materials are used to make oven gloves?

An insulated hot water tank.

We use insulators, such as cork, for tablemats.

This radiator is filled with hot water. It is made of metal because metal allows heat to pass through it easily.

Using insulators

We use insulators to keep heat out and to keep heat in. We use insulators for oven gloves and for the handles of some saucepans, irons and kettles. That way we do not burn our fingers. A polystyrene cup keeps a drink hot. It also stops you burning your fingers.

We use tablemats as insulators so that we do not mark the furniture with hot plates and dishes.

We use insulating materials around the hot water tanks in our houses to stop the hot water inside from cooling down so quickly.

Questions

1 Why are beefburgers often wrapped in layers of paper and a polystyrene carton? Write an explanation or draw a diagram to show what happens.

2 a Does heat travel from a cold object to a hot one, or from a hot object to a cold one?
  b Why should you use oven gloves to pick up a hot pan?
  c What happens to chocolate when you touch it with your fingers? Explain why.
  d What is the movement of heat through solid objects called?

3 If you had a cup of hot tea and a metal teaspoon, how could you show a friend that metal conducts heat well? Draw a diagram to help your explanation.

Keeping warm with air

Hot objects cool down until they are at the same temperature as their surroundings. Cold objects warm up until they are at the same temperature as their surroundings. A hot object which is well **insulated** stays hot much longer. A cold object which is well insulated stays cold much longer.

Air as an insulator

Still air is a good insulator. Trapping warm air next to your body is a good way of keeping warm. Woollen clothes with lots of air spaces will keep you warm. You can also keep warm by wearing several layers of thin clothing. Each layer traps air.

This ski jacket is filled with fluffy materials that trap air.

In cold weather, birds fluff out their feathers to trap air to keep them warm.

In hot weather, birds squash down their feathers.

How do animals keep warm?

Some animals have fur which traps a layer of insulating air around the animals' bodies. Some animals, such as whales and seals, also have a thick layer of fat (blubber) under their skin to insulate them. Fat is a good insulator.

Polar bears, like most animals that live in cold places, have thick fur.

The fat helps to keep whales and seals warm in the very cold waters where they live. We humans do not have much hair on our bodies. Underneath our skin we too have a layer of fat to help keep us warm.

Houses

In a house we can reduce heat loss (and save fuel and money) by using insulating materials. In some houses the insides of the walls are packed with plastic foam which traps air. Under the roof there is a thick layer of glass fibre that helps to stop heat escaping from the rooms below. Double-glazed windows have two layers of glass with air trapped between them. This means that less heat is lost through the glass.

Questions

1 Which of the materials in the box do you think would make the best insulator to keep a mug of hot chocolate warm? Describe how you would carry out a fair test to compare these different materials.

| newspaper | woollen cloth | cardboard |
| plastic | cotton wool | cotton teatowel |

2 A scientist measured how much heat was lost from an old house. These are the results:

Floor   15%
Roof   25%
Walls   35%
Draughts through
doors and windows   15%

a Which part of the house lost most heat?
b Which parts of the house lost least heat?
c Arrange the parts of the house in order of heat loss, putting the highest first and the lowest last.
d What would you do to reduce the heat loss from each part?

3 Describe what happens to your body when you get cold. Which parts of your body get cold first? What do you do to warm yourself up?

Keeping cool

Thermal insulators can be used to keep things cold. This is useful when you want to stop frozen foods from melting.

Cool food

Some picnic boxes and bags are insulated. They are lined with a layer of insulating material that keeps hot foods hot and cold foods cold. Hot and cold foods should not be put into one of these bags or boxes at the same time, though.

Fridges and freezers keep the food cold inside. The sides and door of the fridge or freezer are insulated to stop warmth from the outside getting in. The door also has a tight seal. By keeping warmth out of the fridge or freezer the food inside stays cool.

These men, who live in Algeria, North Africa, wear loose, white robes.

Cool colours

White and light colours reflect the sun's heat. Loose, white clothes are cool to wear in hot weather. Houses in hot countries are often painted white to keep the insides cool.

These white-painted houses are in Southern Spain where it is hot and sunny.

Cool animals

A fennec fox.

When you sweat, it helps your body cool down. Most other animals cannot sweat. The fennec fox lives in the hot deserts of North Africa. The fox's light-coloured fur reflects a lot of the sun's heat. Its large ears lose a lot of heat to the air and so keep the fox cool.

An elephant also needs to keep cool. Its big ears provide a large area through which heat can leave its body.

Questions

1 Collect pictures of the clothes we wear in hot and cold weather. Compare the two sets of pictures. How are the clothes alike? How are they different?

2 Plan an experiment to see which of two picnic bags keeps food cool the longest. Describe what you would do and what measurements you would take. How would you make your experiment fair?

3 Collect pictures of animals that live in very hot places and very cold places. Mix up the two groups of pictures. How many other ways can you now find of grouping them into sets?

Circuits

Electricity that flows is called an electric **current**. Electricity can be useful only when it flows in a complete **circuit**. Then the electricity can work a bulb, electric motor or other electrical equipment.

Complete circuits

When you connect a bulb and a battery with two pieces of wire, the bulb lights up. You have made an electrical circuit. The electricity flows from the battery's negative (–) terminal, through the bulb, to the positive (+) terminal and through the battery to the negative terminal again. A circuit has no beginning and no end; it has to be a loop. The battery makes the electricity flow and pushes it around the circuit.

Varying the current

You can put more batteries in a circuit. A wire or piece of metal connects the bottom of one battery to the top of the next battery. The more batteries you add to the circuit, the brighter the bulb will shine.

Bulbs are made for a certain number of batteries. If you use too many batteries, the bulb will shine brightly but 'burn out' quickly. If it is connected to too few batteries, a bulb will give only a dim light.

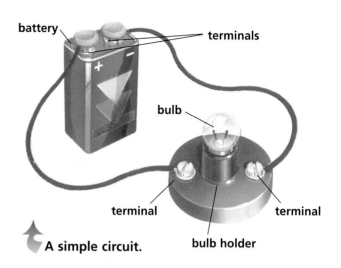

A simple circuit.

Switches

An electric current cannot flow across a gap. In order to turn an electric light on, you usually use a **switch**. A switch works by forming a bridge or gate across a gap in the circuit.

If the switch is in the 'off' position, there is a gap in the circuit and the electricity cannot flow. The light is off. If the switch is in the 'on' position, then the circuit is complete and the electricity can flow.

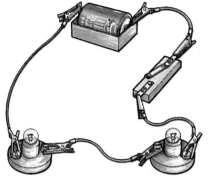

In a series circuit, the electricity flows from the battery through each of the bulbs in turn, and then back to the battery when the switch is closed.

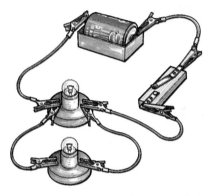

When bulbs are connected in parallel, they each have a separate circuit and some electricity flows through each bulb when the switch is closed.

What happens if you put extra bulbs in the circuit? The pictures show different ways of doing this.

Series circuits

The bulbs in the **series circuit** are not very bright because they are sharing the electric current. Each bulb in the circuit uses some of the electric current flowing around the circuit, and so there is less electricity for each of them. If you add a third bulb there will be even less electric current and the bulbs will be even dimmer. A disadvantage with series circuits is that, if one bulb breaks, the whole circuit stops working.

Parallel circuits

The bulbs in a **parallel circuit** are brighter than they are in a series circuit and if one bulb breaks the others stay alight. The electric lights in your home or school are connected in parallel.

Questions

1 a In your own words describe how a simple switch works. Draw diagrams to show what is happening.

 b Some houses have special switches in them called time switches. Find out what these switches do. Where are time switches used in town and village streets?

2 Draw a plan of a doll's house with four rooms. Put a light in each of the rooms.

On your plan show how you would link up the four bulbs to one battery. What problems will you have in lighting the four rooms separately? Make your circuit to see if it works.

3 Plan an experiment to measure how brightly a torch bulb will shine. Write or draw what you would do. Try it. Record your findings. Was your test fair?

Electrical conductors and insulators

Electricity can flow through some materials but not through others. The wires on an electricity pylon are made of aluminium. Electricity can flow through aluminium. We say that aluminium is a good **conductor** of electricity.

Good conductors

Metals, such as copper and iron, are good conductors of electricity. So is the non-metal graphite which is used in pencil 'leads'. Other conductors include water, damp air, and anything that is wet.

Which other materials could be used as insulators on this electricity pole?

Insulators

Electricity cannot flow through many materials. On an electricity pylon there are large porcelain or glass discs. They stop the electric current in the wires from flowing into the metal pylon and down to the ground. Materials that stop electricity flowing are called **insulators**.

Many common materials are electrical insulators. Plastics, rubber, wood, cloth, glass and paper are electrical insulators. Electricity does not pass through them easily. Bricks, ceramics and dry air are also insulators.

Televisions use a lot of electricity. Plastic coverings are insulators and help to keep us safe.

Using insulators

In our homes and schools, wires carrying electricity are covered in plastic. This is so that the electricity does not pass through anyone who touches them. If the wires were bare and they touched each other, electricity could cross from one wire to another and would not go where it was needed. It might even cause a fire. To stop this happening, the wires are covered with an insulator such as plastic or rubber. Electric plugs and sockets are also made of plastic.

Many electrical 'wires' are really lots of wires bundled together. This is called a **cable**.

An electric cable. The wires have plastic coverings to stop electricity crossing from one wire to another.

Questions

1 a Why is electricity in towns carried by underground cables?
  b Why is electricity often carried across country areas on tall pylons?
  Discuss these questions with friends.

2 Imagine you have made a circuit with a battery, bulb and wires but there is a gap between the ends of two of the wires. If you placed each of the objects listed in the box across the gap, say whether or not you think the bulb would light up.

> matchstick   iron nail   plastic spoon
> piece of cooking foil   pencil
> coin   drinking straw   paper clip
> piece of cardboard

3 True or False? Copy out these sentences. Against each one write True if you think it is correct, or False if you think it is wrong.
  a Materials that stop electricity flowing through them are called electrical insulators.
  b Electricity cannot flow through aluminium.
  c Electrical wires are often made of copper because copper is shiny.
  d Plastic, rubber and glass are good insulators of electricity.
  e Graphite is a good conductor of electricity.

Slowing down

When you ride a bicycle along a level surface, it keeps going as long as you keep pedalling. As you push on the pedals, you make the bicycle's back wheel go round. If you stop pedalling, the bicycle will slow down and stop.

A sliding book

When you push a book across a table, the book will not slide far. Unless you push the book hard, it will slow down and stop before it reaches the other side of the table.

Friction

The bicycle and the book slow down because of a force called **friction**. Friction tries to stop things sliding against each other.

The rougher two surfaces are, the greater the force of friction between them. That is why it is easier to push a toy car across a smooth floor than it is across a rough carpet.

Look at the pictures on the left. Which things are sliding past other things? Which surfaces are rubbing against each other?

Questions

1 Caroline and Michael drew a line across a sloping plank of wood near its top. Michael put the front of his toy car against this line. Then he let the car go. Michael's car travelled 216 cm. When Caroline did the same thing, her car travelled 257 cm.

 a On which of the two cars was the force of friction greatest – Caroline's or Michael's?

 b What made the cars stop rolling?

2 Caroline rolled a toy car down a sloping plank of wood. Then she covered the plank with carpet and rolled the car again. Then she covered the plank with sandpaper and rolled the car down the slope. On which surface did the car travel slowest? Why was this?

3 a What is the name of the force that gives us grip?

 b What sort of surface should a slide have so that you could go down it really fast?

 c Why do we have a good grip on our shoes?

 d Why is it easier to run across grass than it is along an icy pavement?

 e Why do car and lorry tyres have deep treads?

Harmful friction

Friction can be a great nuisance. When one moving part of a machine rubs on another, friction slows the parts down. They gradually wear out and they may squeak while they are rubbing together. That is why machines are oiled. The oil makes surfaces slide over one another more easily so there is much less friction.

We need to oil some parts of a bicycle so that surfaces slide over each other more easily.

Wearing out

Clothes and shoes wear out because of friction. They wear thin when they rub against furniture or the floor. Tyres wear out as they rub against the road. Even the paint on fast jet aircraft is rubbed off by the air rushing past as the aircraft flies along.

The soles of shoes wear out because of friction between the sole and the ground.

Friction and heat

Friction produces heat. On a cold day, you can warm up your hands by rubbing them together. The heat is caused by friction between the palms of your hands. The harder you push your hands together and the faster you rub, the warmer your hands get.

Friction and car engines

In a car engine, friction tries to slow down moving parts that rub together. This wastes fuel. It also produces so much heat that the parts melt.

To reduce friction, the moving parts of the engine are bathed in oil. To reduce the heat that is produced, most car engines have a pump that pushes water around channels inside the engine. The water gets hot as it cools the engine. This hot water then passes to the car's radiator where the cool air passes over it. The air takes away some of the heat before the water returns to the pump.

put oil in here

put water in here

radiator

water pump

A car engine needs oil and water to work properly.

Questions

1 It is quite easy to unscrew the top of a bottle if your hands are clean and dry. It is difficult to unscrew the top of a bottle if your hands are wet and soapy. Why is this? Explain it in your own words.

2 Prehistoric people used to make fire by quickly turning a dry twig in a hole in a wooden block. They put dry grass around the twig, and the grass caught fire. What happened to cause the grass to catch fire?

3 Make a list of all the things which wear out because of friction. Compare your list with the lists your friends have made.

Useful friction

Friction can be a nuisance, but it can also be useful. If there were no friction at all you would not be able to walk or run. Friction allows your shoes to grip the ground.

Without friction nothing would grip.

Striking a match

When we rub the head of a match against the rough strip on the side of the box, friction heats the chemicals in the head of the match and in the rough strip. It makes the match head catch alight.

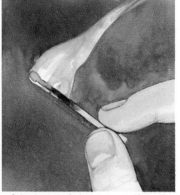

We use the heat produced by friction when we strike a match.

Getting a grip

Without friction, nails and screws would not grip in wood, but would just fall out. You would not be able to ride a bicycle. The wheels would just spin around and not grip the road. Even if you could start the bicycle moving, you would not be able to stop it. This is because the brakes would not grip on the wheels to stop them going around.

Bicycle brakes.

Without friction, you would not be able to write or draw with a pencil or crayon. When you use a pencil or crayon, friction makes some of the pencil 'lead' or crayon wax rub off on to the paper.

Increasing friction

Sometimes we need to increase the amount of friction. Grit is often spread on icy roads to make the road surface rougher. The grit increases the friction between tyres and the road so that tyres grip the road better.

Tractors and snowploughs have tyres with large, deep treads or grooves. These produce a lot of friction and give the tyres a good grip on slippery surfaces. In some countries, where there is a lot of snow and ice in winter, drivers put special chains over their car and lorry wheels to increase the amount of friction on slippery, snow-covered roads.

You slip on an icy path because there is almost no friction between your shoes and the ice-covered ground.

Questions

1 a When you write with a pencil what forces (pushes and pulls) are you using?
   b Is friction being useful or a nuisance when you write with a pencil?
   c Why does the pencil have to be sharpened from time to time?

2 Why is it easier to slip and fall on a wet, tiled floor than it is on a dry one? Describe what happens in your own words.

3 Mr Brown was watering his garden. He had been filling his watering can from the tap. He thought he would save time by fitting a length of hose to the tap. He asked his friend to turn the tap on and off. Then he filled his watering can from the end of the hose, but the watering can took much longer to fill, so Mr Brown had not really saved any time. How did friction make the watering can take longer to fill from the hose than it did from the tap?

Moving through air and water

A bicycle slows down because of the friction between its tyres and the road and because of the friction between its other moving parts. When you ride a bicycle, the friction between the air and the bicycle and you also slows you down. Imagine riding a bicycle through deep water. **Air resistance**, as it is called, is like that, but not nearly so bad!

Streamlining

Racing cyclists wear tight clothes and specially shaped helmets. That makes the air flow around them more easily, so reducing the air resistance. This is called **streamlining**.

Friction can be both useful and a nuisance when you ride a bicycle.

Aircraft and fast cars are streamlined so that the air flows around them more easily. This also saves fuel. The space shuttle is streamlined. Even so, because it is travelling very fast as it approaches the Earth, the air rubbing against the outside of the space shuttle heats it to over 1000°C. This is enough to make it red-hot.

This aircraft is streamlined so that it can fly at 2173 kilometres per hour.

Some very fast jet aircraft use a parachute to help them stop more quickly.

Increasing friction

Sometimes we want to increase the air resistance. A parachute is shaped like a huge mushroom. It pushes against the air as it moves downwards. This causes the parachute to slow down.

Moving through water

Water, like air, slows things down that move through it. Fish have streamlined bodies that move easily through the water. Boats and ships are streamlined so that water flows around them smoothly, reducing friction.

Questions

1 How many things can you think of that are designed to move through the air?
a Draw each of the things.
b How do they move?
c How many ways can you group them into sets?

2 As a spacecraft returns to Earth it is travelling very fast. When the spacecraft enters the Earth's atmosphere it becomes very hot. Why is this?
a In your own words, describe what happens.
b Find out what is done to protect the astronauts inside the spacecraft.

3 Ali and Samantha made model parachutes. Ali used a piece of thin cloth 30 cm by 30 cm. Samantha used a piece of the same cloth 45 cm by 45 cm. They both used the same kind of string. They each tied a plastic cotton-reel to their parachute. The children dropped their parachutes from the same height at the same time. Which parachute do you think took the longest to reach the ground? Say why.

Finding a home

Always put organisms back in the place where you found them.

All living things, both plants and animals, are called **organisms**. The places where groups of organisms live are called **habitats**. Habitats are all different sizes. Woods, hedges, fields, ponds and seashores are habitats. Each is home to many different organisms.

Large and small habitats

A hedge is a habitat for many plants and animals.

Large habitats, like woods and forests, are made up of many smaller habitats. Each type of tree in a wood or forest is a habitat for certain organisms. The rotting logs and branches on the floor of the wood or forest are another habitat. The thick layer of dead leaves on the ground is another. The soil in a wood or forest is home to many more organisms.

Plants, animals and habitats

Plants need the right kinds of soils if they are to grow. They need water and a suitable temperature. They also need a certain amount of sunlight. Many mosses and ferns can live with very little sunlight; most other plants need a lot of sunlight if they are to live and grow well.

A meadow that has not been disturbed by people can be a home to many different plants which are food for certain animals.

Plants may need animals, such as bees and other insects, to carry their pollen from flower to flower so that fruits and seeds can be produced.

Many animals live on plants, so the type of plants growing in a habitat will affect which kinds of animals live there. Certain animals carry fruits and seeds to new places where the plants can grow. Animals, in turn, choose a habitat where they can find food, shelter and be safe from their enemies. The habitat can be a safe place where animals produce young.

Adaptation

Organisms are **adapted** to their habitat. This means that, over thousands of years, each **species** has developed special features to suit the **environment** in which it lives. Squirrels, for example, live in woods and forests. A squirrel has strong back legs to help it climb. It also has sharp teeth for opening nuts and a bushy tail to help it balance on the tree branches.

Questions

1 What is a habitat? Explain it in your own words. Begin your sentence, 'A habitat is ... '.

2 Choose a habitat near your school. Draw the organisms you find there. Find out about them. Which animals eat plants that grow in the habitat?

3 Think about each of the animals and their habitats in the list below. How is each animal adapted (suited) to its environment?
   a fish / water
   b polar bear / Arctic
   c camel / desert
   d earthworm / soil

Living together

Eating is a necessary part of living. Most animals spend much of their time hunting for food or feeding. Plants make their own food. They are called **producers**.

In fact, plants make food for all the animals in the world. Because animals eat plants, or other animals, they are called **consumers**.

Herbivores and carnivores

Many animals eat plants. Horses, elephants, cows, sheep, deer, rabbits and snails are just a few of the animals which eat plants. Without plants, these plant-eating animals, called **herbivores**, would die.

If all the herbivores in a habitat died, the meat-eating animals, or **carnivores**, would have no food, and so they would die. So plants are important to meat-eaters as well as to plant-eaters. All animals depend upon plants, either directly or indirectly, for food.

Which of these animals are herbivores? Which are eaten by other animals?

Food chains

Herbivores eat plants. Herbivores in turn are eaten by carnivores. Those carnivores may be eaten by bigger carnivores. This is called a **food chain**, and we write it like this:

plant ➜ herbivore ➜ 1st carnivore ➜ 2nd carnivore

Food chains always begin with plants. The arrow means 'gives food to'.

Here is a food chain you might find near your home or school. A snail might eat a cabbage leaf in a garden. Then the snail might be eaten by a thrush. The thrush may be eaten by a sparrowhawk. The food chain is:

cabbage ➜ snail ➜ thrush ➜ sparrowhawk

Questions

1 Write and draw some food chains that begin with grass. What do you notice about the size of the animals as you go along a food chain?

2 Think of some food chains that include you. Draw them.

3 What do you think would happen to the plants in a habitat if all the herbivores were killed? What would happen to the plants and herbivores if all the carnivores were killed?

4 Cut out pictures of plants, herbivores and carnivores from magazines. With your friends, arrange your pictures into food chains. Stick your pictures on to a large sheet of paper and make a wall chart.

Life in the school grounds

The environment of the school grounds contains many habitats for plants and animals. Many organisms live on school lawns, playing fields, hedges or flowerbeds. Dark corners and out-of-the-way places, such as store sheds and boiler houses, may provide homes for mice, spiders and other small animals. Even a wall around a school can be a favourite habitat for organisms.

Life on a wall

The older and more crumbly the wall, the more organisms there are likely to be living on it. In one investigation, scientists found more than 185 different organisms living on a wall.

When it is shady and damp, a wall often has a coating of green slime made up of tiny plants called **algae**. Slugs and snails often feed on the algae. If the wall is crumbly, lichens and mosses may grow on it. These plants can slowly dissolve away the mortar holding the bricks together. Then larger plants, such as grasses, stonecrop and ivy, can grow.

Small ferns grow on this damp, shady wall.

Wallflowers are suited to growing in the crevices in a wall.

Spiders often live in crevices in old walls. This wolf spider is carrying her egg cocoon with her.

Crevices in the wall are a home for woodlice, centipedes, millipedes, springtails and beetles. These are hunted by spiders, mice and birds. Animals that eat other animals are called **predators**. So spiders, mice and birds are predators. The animals that the predators kill are called their **prey**. In this case, woodlice, centipedes, millipedes, springtails and beetles are prey.

Sunbathing

On a sunny day, butterflies, bluebottle and greenbottle flies, grasshoppers and hoverflies may rest on the wall. They let the sun warm them up so that they can then move away quickly. Other small animals, such as spiders and centipedes, will hunt and catch these sunbathers.

Questions

1 Ravi and Sara were finding out which animals lived under large stones and bricks. They discovered 11 woodlice, 3 slugs and 4 earthworms. Why might these animals have chosen to live under large stones and bricks? Write down three reasons.

2 How many ways can you think of in which earthworms are suited to life in the soil?
   a Think of their colour.
   b Think of their shape.
   c Think of their food – leaf litter.
   d Think of how earthworms move.

3 Here is a food chain you might see in the school grounds.
   leaf ➜ caterpillar ➜ blackbird ➜ cat
   a Name the producer and draw it.
   b How many consumers are there?
   c Name the prey of the blackbird and draw it.
   d Name the prey of the cat and draw it.
   e What is the predator of the caterpillar?
   f What is the predator of the blackbird?
   g Which animal has no predators in this food chain?

Life in a pond

There are ponds in gardens, parks and city squares, and on farms. You can find ponds high on hills and mountains. All ponds have still water. Usually the pond is shallow enough for sunlight to reach the bottom. This allows plants to grow in the water.

Many species of plants are suited to life in a pond.

yellow flag iris

rushes

water plantain

arrowhead

water forget-me-not

duckweed

water lily

marsh marigold

water crowfoot

water milfoil

Canadian pondweed

Water plants

There are many water plants in sunny ponds. Some, such as duckweed and water fern, are small and float on the surface. Others, like water milfoil and Canadian pondweed, are rooted in the bottom of the pond. Water crowfoot and arrowhead have some leaves below water and some above the surface. Water lilies have large leaves that float on the surface. Open ponds usually have plants, such as rushes, reeds, yellow flag iris and water forget-me-not, growing around their edges.

The frog is adapted to life in the water and in moist places on land.

Pond animals

Many animals feed on the water plants. Water snails, mayfly nymphs and newly hatched frog and toad tadpoles feed on water plants. These herbivores in turn are food for carnivores. The carnivores in a pond include water beetles, water spiders, dragonfly nymphs, pond skaters, sticklebacks and pike.

Scavengers

The lives of the organisms in a pond are linked together by many food chains. Some of the animals in a pond are also **scavengers**. They eat dead leaves, dead animals and the droppings of animals. They help to keep the pond clean. Water skaters, sludge worms and water shrimps are scavengers. The carnivores in the pond may eat these scavengers.

Questions

1 Collect pictures of ponds and pond animals. Think about them carefully.
   a Which animals live in the water all the time?
   b Which animals can fly?
   c Which animals might visit the pond to drink?
   Write their names or draw pictures.

2 Look at the plants living in and around the pond in the picture.
   Copy the list of words below. Circle two things that all these plants need to stay alive and healthy.

   walls   light   soil   fields   water

3 Here are the names of some pond animals:

   frog   newt   dragonfly   stickleback
   pond snail   water skater

   a Which of these animals spend all their lives in pond water? Which spend only part of their lives in water?
   b Find out how each of these animals is suited to its environment.
   c Which of these animals are herbivores? Which of them are carnivores?

Life on the seashore

Where the land meets the sea is called the shore. Not all seashores are sandy. Some are muddy, and some are covered with small stones called shingle, large stones called pebbles, or huge pieces of rock. Some seashores have high cliffs behind them.

Fur seals are adapted to a life spent hunting for fish in the sea.

Tides and waves

Tides and **waves** keep the seawater moving. Twice each day the level of the water in the sea rises. The sea covers the shore. Waves may crash against the rocks and cliffs. We say that the tide is in. Twice each day the level of the sea falls. The seashore and seaweeds are uncovered. We say that the tide has gone out.

If you walk along a beach when the tide is out, you will see few living things, but there are animals in the sand. Cockles and razorshells live below the sand. They put out little tubes from their shells when the tide is in. They get little bits of food from the seawater. Lugworms and sand mason worms also live in the sand. They too feed when the tide is in.

Limpets are adapted to life on rocks that are uncovered at low tide.

Rock pools

When the tide is out, many seaweeds are uncovered in the pools. Some animals are also left in the pools. Prawns and shrimps are often found in rock pools. So are blennies and pipe fish. Other animals, such as crabs, hide under the rocks. All of these animals have to stay where they are until the tide comes in. If they dry out, they quickly die.

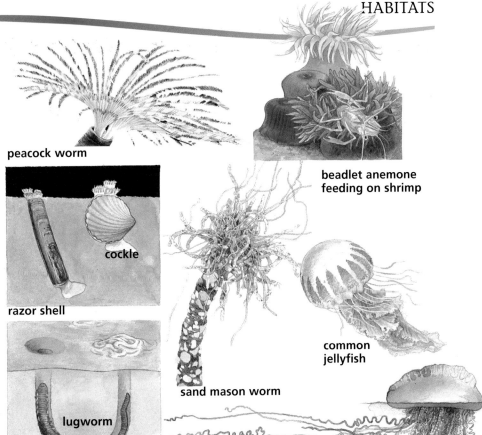

peacock worm

cockle

razor shell

lugworm

beadlet anemone feeding on shrimp

common jellyfish

sand mason worm

Portuguese man o' war

Questions

1 Classify this list of seashore organisms into plants and animals:

> sea anemone   sponge   crab
> seaweed   prawn   alga   pipe fish
> shrimp   cockle   razor shell

Make a table with two columns for your classification. Which group is the largest?

2 Sophie went to look at a rock pool. She watched as a shrimp ate tiny pieces of seaweed. Suddenly a sea anemone shot out its tentacles and caught the shrimp. Which of the living things that Sophie saw was a plant, which was a herbivore and which a carnivore?

Write or draw a food chain for what happened in the rock pool.

3 Look at the picture of limpets living on a rock on the seashore. Limpets are animals that live in shells. When the tide is in they move around to feed on tiny plants that cover the rocks. When the tide is out the limpets stick firmly to rocks. It is almost impossible to pull a limpet from a rock with your fingers.
a What makes a limpet well suited to living in a rock pool?
b How many more rock pool animals can you think of which have shells? What do these animals feed on?

Glossary

Adapted A plant or animal that is suited to its environment.

Air resistance Friction between air and a moving object.

Algae Simple plants, without proper roots, stems or leaves, that live in damp places, fresh water or the sea.

Bone One of the hard parts of an animal's body which makes up its skeleton.

Cable Several wires bundled together.

Carnivore Any animal that feeds on the flesh of other animals.

Celsius scale A scale of temperature on which water freezes at 0°C and boils at 100°C. Named after its inventor, Anders Celsius.

Circuit The complete path of an electric current around a series of wires and connections from a battery or mains socket.

Classify To group things into sets.

Conductor A material that allows heat or electricity to pass through it easily.

Consumer A living thing (usually an animal) which consumes food it has not produced.

Contract To become shorter or smaller.

Current The flow of electricity along a conductor.

Decant To carefully pour off liquid from a solid settled at the bottom of a container.

Degrees Units of temperature.

Dissolve To make a solid substance break up and disappear into a liquid. Together they make a solution. Gases can also be dissolved in a liquid.

Environment An animal's or plant's surroundings.

Evaporate When a liquid turns into a gas as it is heated.

Expand To take up more space.

Filter To separate an insoluble solid from a liquid by passing it through a fine strainer; something used to separate an insoluble solid from a liquid.

Food chain A series of organisms, starting with a green plant, that depend on each other for food.

Freeze To turn a liquid into a solid by cooling. Also called solidifying.

Friction The force that slows down movement and produces heat when two surfaces rub together.

Gas One of the three states of matter. A substance that has no shape and can spread everywhere. Air is made up of a mixture of different gases.

Habitat The place where a plant or animal usually lives.

Herbivore An animal that feeds mainly on roots, fruits, leaves or seeds of plants.

Insoluble Will not dissolve.

Insulate To cover something to keep it hot or cold for longer or to stop electricity from passing through.

Insulator A material that does not allow heat or electricity to pass through it easily.

Joint A place where two moveable parts of an animal's body meet. In humans, and most other animals, it is where the bones in the skeleton meet. The elbow, ankle and knee are joints.

Liquid One of the three states of matter. A substance that can be poured and which spreads out to take the shape of its container.

Marrow The soft substance found inside bones which produces red blood cells.

Melt To change from a solid to a liquid state using heat.

Melting point The temperature at which a substance begins to change from a solid to a liquid.

Muscle One of the parts of the body that contracts to produce movement.

Organism A living thing. All plants and animals are organisms.

Oxygen A gas found in the air. All living things need to take in oxygen to live.

Parallel circuit An electrical circuit that splits into branches and joins together at each end. Each part receives the same amount of electricity.

Predator An animal that eats other animals and catches its food by hunting (also called a carnivore).

Prey One of the animals killed and eaten by a predator.

Producer A green plant which uses energy from the sun to make its food so that it can grow and reproduce.

Relax To rest and recover after exercise; the opposite of contract.

Scale A way of measuring things. A temperature scale is measured in degrees.

Scavenger An animal that eats dead animals and plants.

Series circuit A type of electrical circuit in which all the parts are joined, one after the other, so that the electric current is shared by them.

Skeleton The hard frame that gives the body its shape and protects its soft organs.

Solid One of the three states of matter. Solids keep their shape unless a force is applied to them.

Solidify To turn a liquid into a solid by cooling. Also called freezing.

Solution A liquid in which one or more solutes are dissolved.

Solvent The liquid in which a solute will dissolve.

Species A particular group of animals or plants that are related in some way.

Spinal cord A cord of tissue that connects nerves from all parts of the body to the brain. It is enclosed in the backbone.

States of matter Solid, liquid and gas are the three states of matter.

Streamlined An object or the body of an animal that is built so that it moves smoothly through air or water.

Switch A device used in an electrical circuit to turn the current 'on' or 'off'.

Temperature A measurement of how hot or cold something is.

Tendon A cord of tissue that joins a bone to a muscle.

Terminal The parts of a battery to which the wires are connected in a circuit.

Thermal To do with heat.

Thermometer An instrument that is used to measure temperature.

Tide The regular rise and fall of the surface of the oceans and seas.

Wave A raised ridge of water along the surface of an ocean, sea or large lake caused by the wind blowing on the water.

Index